Original title:
Candles and Snow-Kissed Windows

Copyright © 2024 Creative Arts Management OÜ
All rights reserved.

Author: Isabella Rosemont
ISBN HARDBACK: 978-9916-94-424-0
ISBN PAPERBACK: 978-9916-94-425-7

Heartfelt Warmth Meets the Winter's Chill

In the still of night, the snowflakes fall,
Whispering secrets, a blanket for all.
Fireside glow, where memories stir,
Embers dancing, hearts begin to purr.

Wrapped in blankets, we sit side by side,
Sharing stories, with nothing to hide.
Laughter echoes, a sweet melody,
In this moment, we feel so free.

Through frosty windows, the world seems bright,
Outside is cold, but inside's alright.
Cup in hand, warmth flows through me,
Love's embrace, like a winter's spree.

So let the winter bring all its chills,
We'll find comfort where warmth fulfills.
Together we'll face whatever may come,
In each other's arms, forever we're home.

Shimmers in the Frosted Glow

In the morning light, they gleam,
Frosty patterns like a dream.
Nature's jewels, pure and bright,
Adorning branches in soft white.

A whisper of cold in the air,
Yet beauty blooms, beyond compare.
Glorious sights in the crisp day,
A fleeting moment, then they sway.

Soft Radiance Amidst the Chill

Beneath a blanket, warmth we find,
Softly glowing, our hearts entwined.
The world outside, a frozen art,
Yet in this space, we feel the heart.

With gentle laughter, dreams take flight,
Illuminated by the soft light.
The chill outside may make us shiver,
But here, with you, we dance and quiver.

Warmth Nestled in Icy Silhouettes

Amidst the trees, silhouettes stand,
Icy laces on the land.
Yet in the hearth, our spirits glow,
Holding warmth through winter's flow.

The fire crackles, stories shared,
Against the cold, none are scared.
Nature sleeps, but we embrace,
Together here, in this warm space.

The Light that Defies the Winter Dark

Beneath a sky so deep and gray,
Tiny sparks of light will play.
Against the night, they shine and gleam,
A flicker of hope, a cherished dream.

Stars twinkle bright in the chilly air,
A reminder of warmth, we find it rare.
The dark may linger, but we ignite,
The light inside, a guiding sight.

Shimmering Lights in a Celestial Chill

Stars glisten bright in the deep black sky,
Whispers of winter in every sigh.
Moonlight dances on frost-kissed ground,
In the quiet night, pure magic is found.

A chill in the air that brings hearts close,
Wrapped in warmth, we let love boast.
Under the shimmering celestial glow,
Dreams awaken, and hopes begin to flow.

Radiant Comfort Beneath Frosty Glare

In winter's grasp, the world is still,
The frosty glare tests our will.
Yet coziness waits in the glowing flame,
Radiant comfort that we still claim.

Through window panes, soft light spills,
Inviting warmth as silence fills.
Cocoa brews, and laughter flows,
In this season, true bliss grows.

Ember-Embraced Frosty Nights

Nights wrapped in blankets, soft and warm,
Embers crackle, breaking the norm.
Outside the frost bites at our play,
Inside we cherish this sweet ballet.

Glimmers of fire dance in our eyes,
While tales unfold 'neath the starlit skies.
Embraced by flame, shadows take flight,
Together we thrive on these frosty nights.

The Warmth of Light Through Icy Veils

A shimmer of light through the icy haze,
Guides us onward, through winter's maze.
    Each flicker reveals a hidden way,
    Promising hope for a brighter day.

Veils of ice drape the world in white,
Yet warmth encircles us, pure delight.
    Together we stand, in unity bright,
    Finding joy in the soft, gentle light.

Scented Warmth on Tranquil Nights

The candles flicker soft and low,
While shadows dance, a gentle flow.
The scent of pine in crisp, cool air,
Wraps the world in its tender care.

Whispers travel through the night,
With every breath, a pure delight.
The stars above begin to gleam,
In this moment, we dare to dream.

Illumined Tales in Winter's Grip

Beneath the quilt of silver white,
We gather close, the firelight bright.
Each crackle sparks a tale to tell,
Of winter's magic, casting a spell.

The frost outside may freeze the ground,
But warmth in hearts is always found.
With laughter woven in the air,
We hold these memories, rich and rare.

The Bright Heart of the Frosty Night

A frosty chill embraces all,
Yet hearts ignite within the hall.
The moonlight bathes the world in grace,
While echoes of joy fill the space.

We sip the warmth from cups held tight,
Finding solace in the night.
Each moment lingers, pure and bright,
The world transformed by winter's light.

Harmony of Frost and Firelight

Frosted windows, sparkling anew,
While flames dance with a vibrant hue.
In this blend of cold and heat,
Our souls converge, a rhythmic beat.

The stories shared through embered glow,
Create a warmth that starts to grow.
Together in this sacred space,
We forge our dreams, our hearts embrace.

Whispering Light in Winter's Embrace

Amidst the snowflakes, soft and white,
A gentle glow breaks through the night.
The whispers call from trees so bare,
Winter's embrace, a serene affair.

The moonlight dances on icy streams,
Casting shadows like frosty dreams.
In this hush, the world feels right,
Wrapped in the warmth of whispering light.

Illuminate the Chilling Night

Stars are twinkling in the deep,
While the world rests, cuddled in sleep.
A lantern flickers, casting cheer,
Illuminating paths so clear.

Each corner glows with a soft hue,
Transforming dark into shades anew.
In this calm, the heart takes flight,
Together we brave the chilling night.

Frosty Reflections and Warmth Within

Mirrors of ice, so still and bright,
Reflecting dreams in soft moonlight.
Though the cold wraps around the skin,
Deep in the heart, there's warmth within.

Glistening branches, a crystal dome,
In this winter, we find our home.
Each breath a mist, a silent vow,
Frosty reflections show us how.

Glow of Serenity in a Silent Storm

Whirling snowflakes swirl and spin,
In the storm's heart, the calm begins.
A glow emerges, both soft and bright,
Serenity found in the darkest night.

Whispers of peace float through the air,
Encasing moments in tender care.
The silent storm sings a gentle tune,
As warmth surrounds beneath the moon.

Warmth Lingers in the Bitter Chill

In the stillness of the night,
Fires crackle, soft and bright.
Cozy corners, whispers low,
Hearts entwined in winter's glow.

Frosty air bites at the skin,
Yet inside, warmth seeps within.
Laughter dances through the room,
Love's embrace dispels the gloom.

Stars above in shimmering rows,
Veil the world with crystal snows.
Every flake a story told,
Of timeless magic, dreams of gold.

As the world outside lies still,
We find joy in winter's thrill.
Hand in hand, through cold we roam,
Finding warmth, we are at home.

Winter's Veil and the Soft Glow

A blanket white on fields does lay,
Covering the earth in soft array.
Underneath, life stirs and waits,
For spring to open all the gates.

Moonlight bathes the trees in sheen,
Silent shadows, softly green.
Every branch, a story spun,
Of cold embraced, of day begun.

Candles flicker in the night,
Casting shadows, warm and bright.
Hearts connected, dreams in flow,
In winter's veil, our spirits grow.

As the world breathes in the chill,
We find strength from love's own will.
Through the frost, our laughter glows,
Together, we compose our prose.

Radiance Against the Winter's Gloom

In the depths where darkness lies,
Hope emerges, brightening skies.
Every dawn, a promise new,
That radiance will break on through.

Snowflakes dance in morning light,
Crystal jewels, pure and bright.
Nature's art, a wondrous sight,
Filling hearts with pure delight.

Through the frost, the sun will reign,
Chasing shadows, easing pain.
In the chill, our spirits rise,
From winter's gloom to painted skies.

Gather 'round the hearth tonight,
Feel the warmth, the shared insight.
In each other's eyes, we see,
That love will bloom, eternally.

Luminous Hues on Icy Canvas

The canvas sprawls in hues so bright,
Brush of winter, pure delight.
Reds and golds through icy blue,
A masterpiece in every view.

Footprints trace the frozen ground,
In silence, beauty can be found.
Nature's breath in every gale,
Whispers soft, a soothing tale.

Through the trees, the sunlight streams,
Cascading down like woven dreams.
Every shadow shares a glow,
In this realm of ice and snow.

As we wander, hand in hand,
We paint our memories on the land.
In the silence, our hearts soar,
Luminous hues forevermore.

Radiant Dreams Behind Frosted Panes

In the still of night, dreams sigh,
Frosted panes catch sweet whispers high.
Moonlight dances on crystal shapes,
Casting visions where silence drapes.

Gentle shadows weave through the air,
Each glimmer holds a soft, secret care.
Time drifts softly, a lullaby's sound,
In fragile worlds where peace is found.

Memories linger, like echoes gleam,
Wrapping the heart in a tender dream.
Behind the glass, the world fades away,
Leaving only the night's gentle sway.

Awake in slumber, where wishes bloom,
Radiant hopes dispel the gloom.
With every breath, the magic stays,
In radiant dreams through frosted rays.

Heartbeats in the Glinting White

Amid the snow, where whispers blend,
Heartbeats echo, a soft ascend.
Each flake falls with a promise sweet,
Crisp and clear, the pulse of feat.

In the hush, the world stands still,
Frosty branches, the heart they fill.
Glistening paths beneath moonlight glow,
Together we wander through frozen flow.

Tender moments drape like a veil,
In every heartbeat, a story to tell.
Glinting white, the world anew,
As snowflakes twirl in a wondrous view.

Holding warmth close beneath the chill,
In every silence, our spirits thrill.
With every step, the journey's bright,
In heartbeats lost, embraced by night.

Enchanted Illumination in the Stillness

In twilight's embrace, shadows creep,
Enchanted dreams begin to seep.
Stars awaken, their glow divine,
Illuminating a path, so fine.

Silent whispers dance in the air,
Each secret carried with tender care.
Night unfolds with a shimmering hue,
A tapestry woven, old and new.

Softly gliding through starry beams,
The stillness enchants, ignites our dreams.
In the still, a magic implied,
Where hearts can flourish and fears subside.

Through every flicker, a story unfolds,
In gentle glimmers, truth beholds.
With the night, we find our embrace,
In enchanted light, we find our place.

Warm Embrace Beneath the Glinting Stars

Beneath the stars, where wishes wait,
A warm embrace, a gentle fate.
Laughter mingles with celestial light,
Wrapping our souls in the fabric of night.

As constellations twinkle bright,
We share our dreams in the cool moonlight.
The universe whispers, secrets profound,
In this embrace, love knows no bound.

Wrapped in warmth, we forget the chill,
Moments captured, time stood still.
With every heartbeat, a promise made,
Under the stars, our fears allayed.

In this night, where wonder glows,
The beauty of love forever flows.
Together we shine, like cosmic sparks,
In a warm embrace, beneath the stars.

Flickering Flames in Winter's Embrace

Flickering flames dance with glee,
Casting shadows on the tree.
Whispers of warmth in the cold,
A story of comfort unfolds.

Crisp air outside, cozy inside,
In fire's glow, we want to hide.
Each spark a wish, a dream, a sign,
In winter's chill, our hearts entwine.

Beneath the stars, the night is deep,
While glowing embers gently weep.
In the stillness, love's embrace,
Igniting hope in this sacred place.

So let the world be cold and gray,
We'll find our joy in this display.
Flickering flames, our guiding light,
Together we'll warm the winter night.

Frosted Glass and Warmth Within

Frosted glass, a world concealed,
A glimpse of warmth that's revealed.
Behind the pane, the laughter flows,
As winter's chill outside bestows.

Soft golden light spills through the cracks,
Harboring love in the quiet stacks.
In the hush, our secrets twine,
Wrapped in warmth, we intertwine.

Each breath against the icy sheen,
A testament to what has been.
In whispered tales and shared delight,
We carve our joy in the night.

Frosted glass holds stories dear,
Of friendship, laughter, and cheer.
Though the world may be cold and stark,
Within our hearts, we hold the spark.

Glimmers Through Frosted Veils

Glimmers peep through frosted veils,
Softly telling winter tales.
A dance of light in muted hues,
All is still, the night ensues.

Beneath the stars, the silver glows,
In nature's art, the magic flows.
Each twinkle paints a scene so bright,
A symphony of sheer delight.

The world outside in slumber deep,
While dreams within begin to seep.
In every spark, a wish takes flight,
Embracing warmth in fading light.

Glimmers fade, yet never cease,
In winter's heart, we find our peace.
Though shadows play and darkness calls,
The light of love forever falls.

Whispers of Light on Chill-Blanketed Nights

Whispers of light in the moon's soft glow,
Painting the night with a gentle flow.
A chill blankets all, yet warmth remains,
In subtle gestures, love explains.

Stars glimmer high, like thoughts unspoken,
In the quiet, bonds unbroken.
Each sigh a promise, each laugh a song,
In winter's embrace, we all belong.

Frost-kissed air wraps round our hearts,
In this stillness, the magic starts.
Every shadow holds a tale,
And warmth endures as we set sail.

So let us chase the winter's night,
With whispers of love and soft delight.
In every moment, together we stand,
Whispers of light, hand in hand.

Flames Dance Against Winter's Breath

In the quiet of the night,
Fire warms the frozen ground.
Shadows flicker, spirits bright,
Nature sings a hushed sound.

Whispers of the embers glow,
Casting dreams on frosty air.
The world wrapped in crystal snow,
Yet the heart's warmth is rare.

Dancing flames in subtle sway,
Melting frost with tender grace.
Amidst the cold's cold display,
Hope finds its rightful place.

Winter's breath can chill the bone,
But within we fight the freeze.
Together, never alone,
We embrace the warming breeze.

Glistening Glass and Amber Flame

In the hearth, our fears ignite,
Amber glow against the glass.
Life refracted, dark to light,
Moments fleeting, none can pass.

Winter's cloak wraps all around,
Yet inside, warmth softly gleams.
Glistening in a world bound,
We awaken, chase our dreams.

Fires crackle as night falls slow,
Each flicker tells a tale anew.
Through glassy panes, soft lights flow,
Reminders of the love we knew.

A dance of shadows on the wall,
Reflecting treasures from the past.
In every flame's rise and fall,
Enduring love forever lasts.

Soft Light Reveals the Winter's Secret

Beneath the snow, the earth dreams,
Soft light whispers secrets near.
Hidden truths in moonlight beams,
Winter's heart, both cold and clear.

Trees stand guard in silent grace,
Branch and bough in quiet awe.
Time unveils, at its own pace,
Frosted paths we gently draw.

Glimmers dance upon the frost,
Each step reveals a hidden tale.
In this world where warmth is lost,
Fragile echoes never pale.

Winter's secret, soft and bright,
Lives in moments we hold dear.
In the stillness of the night,
Hope and love are ever near.

Embers of Hope in Frost's Grasp

Frosty whispers linger long,
Embers glowing in the chill.
Winter's night may feel so strong,
But hope thrives beyond the thrill.

Quiet hearts breathe warmth and light,
Fueling dreams beneath the snow.
Together we withstand the night,
With a flame that's sure to grow.

Through the frost, our spirits soar,
Each ember tells a story true.
Rising softly, we explore,
Finding paths of morning dew.

In the dark, our fires hum,
Casting shadows, fierce yet kind.
With each beat, the warmth will come,
Embers of hope we'll always find.

Whispered Hues Beneath a Silver Sky

Soft murmurs drift on gentle breeze,
Colors blend in whispers with ease.
Clouds above in muted sway,
A canvas painted dreams of gray.

Petals sigh in tranquil grace,
Nature's breath, a warm embrace.
Shadows dance beneath the glow,
Whispers of a world below.

The twilight dips in sapphire hue,
Painting silence, deep and true.
Stars awaken with a spark,
Illuminating all the dark.

Each moment holds a fleeting light,
A melody of day and night.
In every hue, a story lies,
Whispered softly 'neath the skies.

Remnants of Warmth in the Crisp Air

Autumn leaves in swirling flight,
Crimson whispers, pure delight.
Chill bites softly at the skin,
Yet warmth of sun still lingers in.

Fires crackle with old tales,
Echoes of laughter drift in gales.
Blankets wrap in cozy folds,
Holding secrets long retold.

Sips of cider, spiced and sweet,
Gathering friends, a cherished treat.
In every breeze, a quiet cheer,
The dance of warmth, although austere.

As twilight paints the world anew,
Remnants of warmth in vibrant view.
In crisp air, memories blend,
A haunting call that won't soon end.

The Dance of Light Against the Cold

Moonlight waltzes on frozen lakes,
Casting dreams as silence wakes.
Shimmers glide on icy breath,
A tapestry defying death.

Snowflakes twirl in graceful flight,
Catching gleams of silver light.
In the stillness, shadows play,
Night and dawn in soft ballet.

Each sparkle holds a secret bright,
Whispered stories wrapped in light.
Frosted branches beckon soft,
Nature's symphony aloft.

The world awakens, deep and bold,
As light and cold embrace their fold.
In this dance, a tale untold,
Shimmers 'neath the winter's hold.

Enchanted Reflections in Winter's Lullaby

Gentle whispers in the snow,
Nature's lullaby, soft and slow.
Stars retreat from icy skies,
Time stands still, as silence sighs.

Misty breaths on chilly air,
Reflections shimmer everywhere.
Moonbeams kiss the frozen ground,
In this moment, peace is found.

Each flake tells a story bright,
Dancing softly in the night.
Winter's grace wraps all in light,
Holding dreams in purest white.

Awake to magic, pure and clear,
Winter's lullaby draws near.
In enchanted dreams, we rest,
Wrapped in the warmth, we feel the best.

Light Against the Silent Snowfall

Soft whispers dance where snowflakes fall,
A gentle glow beneath it all.
The world in white, so pure and still,
While light ignites the winter chill.

Beneath the branches bowed in grace,
A golden hue finds its place.
Each crystal catches a warm delight,
As day surrenders to the night.

In silence deep, the shadows play,
Yet warmth persists, come what may.
In every flake, a story spun,
Of light and snow, forever one.

The Warmth of Light and the Chill of Winter

The sun peeks through the frosty trees,
A tender touch in the biting breeze.
Each morning dawns with a gentle fight,
As warmth defies the strands of night.

With every breath, the cold snaps back,
Yet joy ignites the barren track.
Together they dance, so sweet, so bright,
In the heart of winter's chilling light.

Fires flicker in the homes we keep,
While outside, the world is fast asleep.
A balance found, warm hearts entwine,
In every chill, the light will shine.

When Light Meets Winter's Embrace

When morning breaks, the world transformed,
A canvas bright, through coldness warmed.
The beams of gold, a soft caress,
Paint winter's chill with tenderness.

Snowflakes shimmer as light descends,
An icy world where warmth transcends.
In every glimmer, a promise made,
That even in cold, the sun won't fade.

Through frozen branches, shadows weave,
A tapestry of love we believe.
In winter's grasp, we stand and see,
How light and chill can set us free.

Serene Glow in the Cold's Caress

In tranquil hush, the snowflakes fall,
A serene glow envelops all.
The cold wraps tight like whispered dreams,
While light flows softly in silver streams.

Each moment lingers, crisp and bright,
As shadows dance in the fading light.
The world holds still in a gentle sigh,
With winter's breath, and the sun up high.

Frozen beauty, a soft embrace,
In twilight's grip, we find our place.
As night unfurls its starry thread,
The glow remains, where hopes are fed.

Dreamscapes of Light in Frozen Realms

In the hush of a winter's night,
Shadows dance with pure delight.
Whispers of snowflakes take their flight,
Creating dreams, like stars, so bright.

Moonlight spills on the frozen lake,
Mirrors of wonder, hearts awake.
Every crystal holds a secret ache,
In this realm, where dreams dare break.

Glistening paths weave through the trees,
Caught in moments, a gentle breeze.
Through this magic, our spirits tease,
Awakening hopes, like whispered pleas.

In frozen realms, the light will play,
Guiding lost souls along the way.
Together we'll chase the night's ballet,
In dreamscapes where our visions sway.

A Glow in the White Stillness

Amidst the white, a soft glow thrives,
Illuminating where stillness strives.
In silence deep, the heart archives,
A moment of peace that gently arrives.

Each flake that falls, a whispered song,
In this white stillness, we belong.
Nature's breath, serene and strong,
In the glow, we find where dreams prolong.

Footprints marked in the pure, bright snow,
Leading us where the warm winds blow.
In that light, our thoughts will flow,
As we embrace what we both know.

With every dawn, the stillness gleams,
A canvas rich with soft white dreams.
In the chill, we find our themes,
Wrapped in warmth, as the sunlight beams.

Traces of Light on Icy Shores

On icy shores where dreams unfold,
The sun dips low, a tale retold.
Waves of light, both brave and bold,
In frozen whispers, secrets hold.

Glimmers play on the chilly ground,
Where shadows dance, and hope is found.
The ocean breathes with a gentle sound,
In this delicate world, love is crowned.

Each reflection tells a journey near,
Of laughter shared and without fear.
In frosty air, we draw so clear,
Traces of warmth, forever dear.

As twilight wraps the world in grace,
We wander through this sacred space.
With every light, we find our place,
On icy shores, our dreams embrace.

Flickering Glow on Frosted Panes

Beyond the glass, a world so bright,
Hopes and dreams take wing in flight.
Frosted panes catch the morning light,
Flickering warmth, a pure delight.

Inside, we gather, spirits soar,
With heartbeats echoing evermore.
Each laugh and story, we explore,
In this glow, we find what we adore.

The winter winds may howl and cry,
But here, beneath the starlit sky,
A flickering glow, we cannot lie,
Keeps us warm when the world is dry.

In every breath, we feel the magic,
Through frosted glass, moments tragic,
Transform to warmth, a joy ecstatic,
In love's embrace, we're fully plastic.

Serenity in a Crystal-Cloaked Haven

In the hush of morning light,
A world wrapped in frosty white.
Whispers of nature softly call,
In this haven, I stand tall.

Glistening crystals on every tree,
A wonderland for me to see.
Silence blankets the frigid air,
Peace enfolds me everywhere.

Footprints crunch on a snowy trail,
With every step, calm prevails.
Serenity dances through the pines,
In this moment, pure love shines.

As twilight drapes its velvet cloak,
The stars above like diamonds poke.
In this crystal haven's embrace,
I find solace in nature's grace.

Chasing Shadows in a Winter's Night

A silver glow on fields so bright,
I chase the shadows, it's pure delight.
The moon hangs low, a watchful eye,
While whispers of the night drift by.

Footsteps echo on the frozen ground,
In this stillness, magic is found.
With every breath, the world feels right,
In the depths of a winter's night.

Stars ignite, a celestial dance,
Enveloped in the night's romance.
Chasing dreams like shadows that flee,
A canvas painted wild and free.

In the frost, I leave my trace,
Each moment filled with endless grace.
Though shadows fade as dawn draws near,
In my heart, this night stays dear.

Flickers and Flurries: A Love Story

Amidst the flurries, our laughter flows,
In every glance, affection glows.
Hands entwined as we twirl around,
In this whirlwind, true love is found.

Flickers of warmth in the icy chill,
Hearts beating fast with the thrill.
Each snowflake kissed by the spark,
A story written in the dark.

With every step, the night ignites,
Illuminated by soft delights.
From whispered dreams to shared delight,
Together, we embrace the night.

As the world fades in quiet grace,
I see forever in your face.
Flickers and flurries intertwine,
In this love story, you are mine.

Winter's Breath and the Firelight's Touch

In the cold, winter's breath does weave,
Stories whispered, no one can leave.
The crackling fire shares its glow,
A warm embrace when outside's below.

Snowflakes dance with a gentle grace,
Winter's chill holds a secret space.
But here beside the flames we find,
Comfort that eases every mind.

As shadows play, time feels so slow,
In this moment, love tends to grow.
With each flicker and every sigh,
Together, we watch the years fly by.

Wrapped in warmth, the world fades away,
In firelight's touch, we choose to stay.
Winter may chill, but hearts ignite,
In our haven of warmth this night.

Glistening Nights and Subtle Sparks

Under the moon's soft gaze,
Stars weave a dance on high.
Whispers of night embrace,
Painting dreams in the sky.

Gentle breezes carry tales,
Of love and light so rare.
With each glistening trail,
Hope flickers in the air.

Shadows play on silver grass,
In the hush of midnight's song.
Each moment seems to pass,
Where hearts and dreams belong.

The Elegance of Light in a Frosty World

Morning light breaks so clear,
Frost drapes the fields in white.
A shimmer of beauty near,
Embracing the chill of night.

Crystal branches gently sway,
Bathed in warmth's tender glow.
In this frosty ballet,
Nature puts on a show.

Silence dances with grace,
The world breathes soft and slow.
A wondrous, serene space,
Where dreams of winter flow.

Quiet Radiance Amidst the Flurry

Snowflakes drift, light as air,
Coating the earth in peace.
A love song whispers there,
As all chaos finds release.

Amidst the storm so bold,
Soft lights begin to gleam.
In the frosty air, behold,
A world kissed by a dream.

Stillness reigns in the night,
Stars twinkle, calm, and bright.
In winter's gentle flight,
Hope rises with the light.

Ethereal Glow Through Frozen Dreams

In the hush of twilight's grace,
A whisper of light arrives.
Casting shadows, it will trace,
The beauty where hope thrives.

A delicate, golden hue,
Spills across the frozen ground.
Every heart feels anew,
In this glow, magic is found.

Through the veil of chilly air,
Dreams awaken, softly stir.
Fragrant life flows everywhere,
In the stillness, we concur.

Twinkling Tiers of White and Warmth

Snow falls gently on the ground,
Layers of white, a soft surround.
In the glow of lantern light,
Warmth embraces the silent night.

Children laugh, their spirits high,
As sparkling flakes drift from the sky.
Footprints mark a joyful path,
In this winter's playful bath.

The world transformed, so pure, so bright,
Underneath the stars' soft light.
In stillness, dreams so softly weave,
A tapestry of hope, believe.

Hearts aglow with love so deep,
In the quiet, secrets keep.
Whispers dance on frosty air,
In twinkling tiers, we find our care.

Celestial Flames Over Winter's Expanse

Stars like embers fill the night,
Celestial flames, a wondrous sight.
Over white fields they gleam and glow,
Guiding hearts where warm winds blow.

The moon, a lantern in the sky,
Illuminates each dream nearby.
Frosty branches catch its beam,
Nature whispers, love's sweet dream.

In silence, magic starts to play,
Every shadow finds its way.
Winter's breath, a soft caress,
Wrapped in love, we find our rest.

Crisp nights filled with starlit grace,
In this wondrous, boundless space.
Celestial flames guide us through,
Winter's heart beats just for you.

The Glow That Defies the Freeze

Amber lights, they sparkle bright,
Chasing away the edge of night.
The chill may bite, but we feel warm,
In this haven, our hearts transform.

Fires crackle, stories unfold,
As embers' tales are sweetly told.
In every glow, a promise stays,
That love will guide our winter days.

The frost may linger, crisp and clear,
Yet we find joy in those we hold dear.
Through frozen paths, our laughter rings,
Like the dance of air on gossamer wings.

So let us toast to warmth and cheer,
In the glow that draws us near.
Through every storm and cold embrace,
We carry light in winter's grace.

Dancing Light Beneath Frosty Stars

Beneath a sky of diamond bright,
We find our dreams in winter's night.
The cold can bite, but hearts ignite,
In dancing light, we take our flight.

Each twinkle shines with tales untold,
In frosty dreams, our souls unfold.
With every breath, the world transforms,
As hearts unite in swirling storms.

Ice and fire, hand in hand,
Creating a magic, so unplanned.
In every twirl, a warmth we find,
As stars above, in joy, remind.

We cast away the chill and fear,
Embracing love that's ever near.
So let us dance, both wild and free,
Beneath the stars, just you and me.

Flickers of Home in Wintry Isolation

The snowflakes dance, a gentle sight,
While shadows stretch, consumed by night.
In corners dim, a candle glows,
Its flicker sings of warmth and close.

The walls embrace, a sturdy frame,
They cradle dreams and whisper names.
Through frosted panes, the world outside,
Hides tales of storms where hearts reside.

In quietude, the moments blend,
Like threads of hope that never end.
Each flicker holds a story spun,
Of futures bright when day is done.

So let the wintry winds be harsh,
Within these walls, our souls can larch.
For in this space, where love is sown,
We find our peace, our flickers of home.

The Soft Glow of Comforting Whispers

In twilight's hush, soft voices twine,
Like gentle breezes through the pine.
Each word a warm and tender hug,
A soft glow in the dark snug.

The hearth is alive, embers flicker bright,
Casting shadows that feel just right.
With laughter shared around the fire,
Time dissolves, our hearts conspire.

Outside the chill, within the glow,
A blanket of warmth, love's undertow.
We share our dreams, the night's embrace,
In whispered tones, we find our place.

So let the winter winds resound,
In this soft glow, we are spellbound.
For in these whispers, dreams do teem,
A world alive, a shared dreamstream.

Tranquil Flames Against Bitter Winds

The world outside is cold and bleak,
Yet here we find what hearts can speak.
The flames are bright, a steadfast friend,
Against the winds, they softly blend.

Each spark that rises, hopes take flight,
In the warmth of this sacred light.
We gather close, like moths to fire,
In whispered tales, we lift each other higher.

Through crackling noise, we share our bliss,
In every glance, in every kiss.
These tranquil flames, they never cease,
To warm our souls and bring us peace.

So let the bitter winds outside,
Remind us of this love and pride.
In every flicker, promises bloom,
In tranquil flames, we find our room.

Warming Hearts Amidst the Winter White

In drifts of snow, the world seems still,
Yet in our hearts, there's warmth to fill.
Hot cocoa brews, the kettle sings,
As laughter echoes, each joy it brings.

Beneath the stars, we find our way,
In crisp, cold air, where shadows play.
Together bound, no chill can bite,
For warming hearts ignite the night.

The winter white may cloak the land,
But here we stand, a loving band.
With every cheer and every smile,
We make the cold seem worth the while.

So let the seasons change and freeze,
For in this life, we find our ease.
With warming hearts, we'll dance and sway,
Amidst the winter, come what may.

Glowing Hearts in Frosty Surroundings

In the chill of winter's breath,
Hearts ignite with warmth beneath.
Snowflakes swirl like whispered dreams,
In the glow of quiet gleams.

Through the frost, our laughter calls,
Echoes dance on icy walls.
Each embrace a fiery spark,
Lighting up the still, dark park.

Candles flicker in the night,
Softening the shivers' bite.
Together, wrapped in love's sweet song,
Where our glowing hearts belong.

Amidst the cold, we will stay,
Chasing shadows far away.
With each heartbeat, warmth we share,
Glowing in the frosty air.

The Dance of Light and Snowflakes

Snowflakes twirl like dancers bold,
In the air, a sight to behold.
Lights above begin to sway,
As the night consumes the day.

Each flake falls with silent grace,
Joining in a dazzling chase.
Twinkling stars join in the fun,
Playing under the winter sun.

Warmth surrounds as shadows play,
In a world of pure ballet.
Light and snow, a perfect pair,
Whispering secrets in the air.

In this dance, our hearts will soar,
As we revel on winter's floor.
Together, in this wondrous night,
Caught in the dance of light.

Wicks of Warmth Amidst the Frost

Candles flicker, hearts entwined,
In the shadows, love we find.
Wicks of warmth against the cold,
Stories of the brave and bold.

Through the frost, their glow persists,
Kissing hands and warming wrists.
Each soft flicker, dreams unfold,
In the night, our hearts consoled.

Wrapped in blankets, close we stay,
Flickering flames lead the way.
In this haven, time stands still,
Wicks of warmth, a gentle thrill.

Moments shared in tender light,
Amidst the frost, a pure delight.
Together, as the shadows play,
Heartfelt warmth to guide our way.

Twinkling Spirits in the Hushed Night

In the hush of silent night,
Twinkling spirits shine so bright.
Stars above, a cosmic dance,
Guiding hearts with every glance.

Snow blankets the world with white,
Softening edges, calm delight.
Each sparkle tells a tale anew,
Of all the dreams we dare pursue.

In the shadows, whispers breathe,
Promises that we will weave.
Hand in hand, we make our way,
Together in this night's ballet.

As the hours gently pass,
Underneath the night's fine glass,
We will cherish every sight,
Twinkling spirits in the night.

Glistening Reflections of Hearth and Flurry

Snowflakes dance in the chilly air,
Fires crackle, a warmth we share.
Light flickers against the window's pane,
In this moment, we feel no pain.

Bright reflections, the world in white,
Fleeting glimpses of pure delight.
Wraps of warmth, we linger near,
In glistening stillness, all is clear.

Whispers of winter, soft and low,
Each breath crystal, a gentle glow.
The hearth, our heart, a safe embrace,
In flurries, we find our place.

With every ember, shadows play,
Binding us in this warm array.
Together we weave in night's retreat,
In reflections sweet, our souls complete.

Embered Hues Against White Drapes

Cocoa steams in mugs held tight,
Outside, the snow gleams ever bright.
Embers dance in the hush of night,
Colors warm as the day takes flight.

Beneath the drapes, a world concealed,
In shades of red, the heart revealed.
The crackling fire, a painter's brush,
Against white canvases, the colors rush.

Twinkling lights adorn the space,
Echoing laughter, a warm embrace.
With every sip, the chill recedes,
In embered hues, the spirit feeds.

As winter whispers a frosty tune,
We cradle warmth beneath the moon.
With candles lit, the night unfolds,
In stories shared, our hearts are bold.

Hushed Glow Beneath a Winter Sky

A blanket of snow, the earth asleep,
Whispers of winds, secrets they keep.
Under the sky, a hush so deep,
In the quiet, our dreams we sweep.

Stars sprinkle lightly, a glimmering sight,
Guiding us softly through the night.
With each breath, a frosty sigh,
Moonlight waltzes as shadows fly.

Trees stand still, their branches bare,
In the stillness, love fills the air.
Through the chill, we find our way,
In hush of night, our worries sway.

Together we walk, hand in hand,
In this winter wonder, we make our stand.
The glow of warmth, a twinkling eye,
In the heart's embrace, we softly lie.

Illuminated Tranquility in a World of White

Glistening snow underfoot we tread,
As tranquil silence is gently spread.
In a world of white, we find our ease,
Wrapped in comfort, as hearts appease.

The lanterns glow a golden hue,
Against the canvas of night so true.
Our laughter dances on icy air,
In illuminated calm, we share.

Branches outlined, a frosted lace,
We wander freely, time holds no race.
With every step, the chill takes flight,
In harmony's glow, all feels right.

As winter settles, the stars align,
In this serene world, our spirits shine.
With nature's touch, we seek to feel,
A tranquil heart, forever real.

Ember Kisses Beneath the Night Sky

In twilight's warmth, the embers glow,
Whispers of love in the soft winds blow.
Stars twinkle bright in the darkened sea,
Echoes of dreams where hearts wander free.

The moonlight dances on gentle streams,
Carrying secrets of long-held dreams.
Crickets serenade the tranquil night,
While shadows weave tales held tight in flight.

Beneath the vastness, we find our place,
Bathed in the glow of a tender embrace.
With every heartbeat, the world fades away,
In ember kisses, together we sway.

Softly the night wraps us in its fold,
As stories of old in our hearts unfold.
Together we drift on this starlit tide,
In the warmth of love, we shall forever bide.

Lanterns Adrift in Winter's Silence

Snowflakes fall softly, a whispering sigh,
Lanterns alight as the night draws nigh.
Glistening paths in the shivering air,
Brought forth by lanterns, so bold and rare.

In frosted stillness, we wander and roam,
Each flickering light leads us gently home.
Shadows cast long by the lantern's glow,
Guiding our steps through the moonlit snow.

A hush envelops the world all around,
As magic weaves softly into the ground.
In every glow, stories are shared,
Of warmth and love, for hearts unprepared.

Together we linger, with hands intertwined,
In the light of the lanterns, our souls defined.
Each ember, a promise that flickers in sight,
Adrift in winter, we bask in the light.

Sparkling Solace Behind Frosted Barriers

Behind frosted windows, the world seems still,
Yet echoes of laughter offer a thrill.
Sparkling solace, a quiet retreat,
Where warmth wraps around like a soft, wool sheet.

In silence, we sip on the sweet cocoa,
Watching the snowfall like soft, drifting glow.
Each flake tells a tale of days long gone,
While hopes for tomorrow linger like dawn.

The fire crackles, a dance in the night,
With every ember, our spirits take flight.
Bound by the calm of the winter's embrace,
Behind frosted barriers, we find our grace.

As stars twinkle brightly beyond winter's breath,
We cherish the moments, defying all depth.
In this cozy haven, love will remain,
Sparkling solace that never wanes.

Glow of Remembrance in Winter's Gaze

In winter's gaze, memories unfurl,
A soft, golden glow that lights up our world.
Echoes of laughter in snowflakes that fly,
Binding our hearts as the moments pass by.

Fireside warmth, where the stories ignite,
Each ember a wish, a promise, a light.
Through chill of the night, we hold on to care,
With every heartbeat, your presence is there.

In the hush of the evening, whispers take flight,
Carried on winds deep within the night.
The glow of remembrance wraps us in peace,
In winter's embrace, our love will not cease.

Together we stand, as the seasons unfold,
With warmth in our hearts, and stories retold.
In winter's vast wonder, we find what we crave,
The glow of remembrance, a love that we save.

The Hearth's Whisper in Frozen Silence

In the stillness of night, the fire glows bright,
Casting shadows that dance with delight.
Outside the world sleeps, wrapped in white,
While warmth envelopes, making it right.

Voices of laughter, a soft, sweet sound,
Echoing gently, love truly found.
The hearth whispers tales as embers go round,
In this space of solace, joy is profound.

Flickers of light in the dark, they twine,
A tapestry woven, a life so divine.
Between hearth and heart, the stars align,
In frozen silence, our spirits entwine.

Embers will fade, yet the warmth remains,
In bitter cold, through joys and pains.
In the echo of flames, love still reigns,
The hearth's soft whisper, where hope sustains.

Gentle Flames Guarding Against the Cold

Gentle flames dance, their glow like a sigh,
Protecting our souls as the winter winds cry.
In the embrace of warmth, time passes by,
Within these moments, our dreams can fly.

The crackle and pop, a comforting tune,
Keeping at bay the night's silver moon.
With every flicker, a promise immune,
Against the chill, like a soft afternoon.

Gathered together, we share in the light,
Each laugh, every story, makes everything right.
In the heart of the hearth, the future seems bright,
As gentle flames guard against the cold night.

Together we sit, with love as our guide,
With flames as our shield, and hope by our side.
In this sacred space, we've nothing to hide,
For together, the warmth is a love stratified.

Winter's Breath on Warming Art

Snowflakes whisper secrets on the canvas so wide,
A world painted white where dreams reside.
Each stroke a memory, love as our guide,
Winter's breath shows us where joys are tied.

With every brush, the colors ignite,
As fires of passion turn shadow to light.
The chill is an artist that sparks our delight,
Creating warm visions in the frosty night.

Songs of the season in colors unfold,
Tales of the heart, both timid and bold.
Crafted with warmth, not bought or sold,
In winter's embrace, our stories are told.

Art from the heart, like flames softly twine,
On this frozen canvas, our spirits align.
With winter's breath, our thoughts intertwine,
Creating a masterpiece, a love divine.

Luminous Memories of Snowy Eves

On snowy eves, the world turns to gold,
As memories shimmer, their warmth we hold.
Each flake a whisper, stories unfold,
In luminous moments, our hearts are consoled.

Crisp air carries laughter, a sweet, tender sound,
Echoes of joy that forever surround.
In the blanket of silence, peace can be found,
While dreams swirl like snow, gently unbound.

We gather with loved ones, creating our lore,
The stories we tell are the ones we adore.
Each smile, every glance, opens a door,
To winters remembered and hopes to explore.

Through frosty windowpanes, we watch the night fall,
As stars wink above us, in their silent call.
In luminous memories, together we sprawl,
Crafting warmth in our hearts, through winter's enthrall.

Glimmers of Joy on Chilly Nights

In the stillness of the night,
Stars twinkle, shining bright.
Frost kisses every tree,
Whispers of joy, wild and free.

Children laugh as snowflakes fall,
Building snowmen, they stand tall.
Hot cocoa warms frozen hands,
In these moments, true bliss expands.

Candles flicker in window panes,
Casting light on snow-laden lanes.
Footsteps crunch on paths of white,
Hearts aglow, pure delight.

Nights like these spark memories,
Glimmers of joy in the winter freeze.
Each breath a cloud, crisp and clear,
Chilly nights bring loved ones near.

Warmth Ignites in a Frozen Realm

Amidst the chill, a fire glows,
Casting warmth where cold wind blows.
Families gather, stories unfold,
In the hearth's heart, love is sold.

Snow blankets the world in white,
Yet within, our spirits ignite.
Laughter rings as embers dance,
In this frozen realm, we take our chance.

With each log, our dreams arise,
Crackling flames and starlit skies.
Weaving tales of warmth and cheer,
In this place, our hearts are near.

Beneath the frost, life's beauty glows,
In winter's grasp, affection grows.
Together we face the night's cold air,
Warmth ignites, as hearts lay bare.

Illuminated Solitude in the Snow

In quiet fields, the snow lies deep,
A blanket silent, where shadows creep.
Moonlight glistens on frozen streams,
Illuminated solitude breeds dreams.

Footprints fade in the frosty haze,
Solitude's gift in the night's embrace.
Whispers of snowflakes, soft and slow,
In this stillness, thoughts freely flow.

Branches bow with their icy weight,
Nature's artwork, serene and great.
In the night, a tranquil song,
Illuminated, where I belong.

Here, in the quiet, I find my peace,
Amidst the snow, my worries cease.
Each breath I take, a moment to savor,
Illuminated solitude, my favorite flavor.

Rhythms of Flames in the Silent Cold

Amidst the hush of winter's night,
Flames dance softly, a flickering light.
The rhythm of fire, a soothing beat,
In the cold, its warmth feels sweet.

Logs crackle, stories intertwine,
In this circle, spirits align.
With each spark, dreams ignite,
In the silent cold, hearts take flight.

Outside, the world wears a frostbit crown,
But here, we gather, never let down.
Embers glow, casting shadows long,
Rhythms of flames where we belong.

As the night deepens, and winds grow bold,
We'll share our secrets, our hearts unfold.
In the embrace of fire's warm hold,
Rhythms of flames in the silent cold.

Waxed Moments Amidst the Chill

Candles glow on tranquil nights,
Whispers dance in soft moonlight.
Frosted panes, a gentle sigh,
Time stands still as moments fly.

Embers warm the silent air,
Memories linger, rich and rare.
Beneath the stars, thoughts intertwine,
In these waxed moments, we find divine.

Snowflakes drift like fleeting dreams,
In the glow, nothing's as it seems.
Hearts entwined in quiet grace,
In the chill, we find our place.

Together here, our spirits soar,
In the silence, we seek more.
Waxed moments etched in the night,
Amidst the chill, love finds its light.

The Spirit of Light in Winter's Hold

When winter's chill enfolds the land,
The spirit of light takes a stand.
Candles flicker, shadows wane,
Bringing warmth through the icy rain.

The hearth glows bright, hearts gather near,
Stories shared, voices clear.
Outside the world is cold and stark,
Inside, we light our tiny spark.

Snow blankets dreams in quiet white,
The spirit dances, pure delight.
Each twinkle shines like a guiding star,
In winter's hold, we've come so far.

Let joy ignite in every soul,
As winter wraps its frosty scroll.
Through this chill, we find our way,
The spirit of light with us will stay.

Hushed Shadows on a Winter's Eve

Hushed shadows creep on winter's eve,
Whispers in the night, we weave.
Beneath the moon's soft silver glow,
Time unfolds like freshly fallen snow.

Footprints fade in the silent night,
Where dreams take flight, hearts feel light.
Each breath a cloud, tender and slow,
In hushed shadows, our secrets grow.

Stars peek through the icy shroud,
Nature sleeps, soft yet proud.
We gather close, a poignant scene,
In the stillness, peace is gleaned.

As the world turns, we ignite hope,
In whispered dreams, together we cope.
Hushed shadows frame our hearts' reprieve,
On this winter's eve, we believe.

The Flicker That Guides Through Snow

The flicker that guides through snow so deep,
Illuminates paths where shadows creep.
Amidst the white, a world anew,
Each glimmer whispers, dwell and pursue.

In frosted fields where silence reigns,
Hope's flame dances, gently remains.
Through biting winds, it softly calls,
Inviting hearts where warmth befalls.

Glimmers of light in a dusky haze,
Lead us forward, in winter's gaze.
The journey may be long and bleak,
But with each flicker, we find our peak.

Step by step, in rhythm, we tread,
Guided by light, not fear nor dread.
The flicker that guides, steadfast and true,
In the heart of winter, finds rest in you.

Flickers of Nostalgia in a Snow-Cloaked World

Whispers of winter dance on the breeze,
Frosted memories, brought to the knees.
Footprints in snow, where we used to roam,
Echoes of laughter, calling us home.

Candles are lit in windows aglow,
Fragrant spices, the warmth we know.
Old songs resound with a tender hush,
Time seems to pause in the soft twilight rush.

Each flake that falls carries tales of old,
Stories as precious as silver and gold.
Flickers of nostalgia, a sweet embrace,
In a snow-cloaked world, we find our place.

Winter's breath lingers, soft as a sigh,
Wrapped in the warmth of a starlit sky.
Moments of wonder, alive in the chill,
A flickering heart, forever will thrill.

The Warm Edge of a Frigid Night

Beneath a blanket of twinkling stars,
Chill in the air, yet warmth from afar.
Firelight dances, shadows do play,
In the stillness of night, dreams softly sway.

Cups filled with cocoa, in hands they reside,
Stories exchanged, side by side.
Laughter rises, cutting the cold,
The warm edge of night, a comfort untold.

Breath puffs like clouds, rising in air,
Sparkling all around, magic to share.
Hearts intertwined in the crackling light,
Together we shine, oh, what a sight!

As the moon casts its glow over the earth,
We find in this moment, the essence of worth.
In the chill of the night, our spirits ignite,
In the warmth of each other, everything's right.

Shards of Light on the Chilled Glass

A world of crystals, shimmering bright,
Sunbeams break through, casting pure light.
Shards on the windows, they dance and entwine,
Each glimmering fragment, a moment divine.

Frost patterns weave like dreams on a pane,
Nature's own art, a delicate chain.
Colors that flicker with every soft sigh,
In the hush of the morning, wonder stands by.

Winter's embrace, a palette of white,
Illuminates shadows, transforms day to night.
Caught in the chill, yet warmth begins to rise,
As shards of light capture the skies.

Innocent joy held in crystalline forms,
Protecting the whispers of soft winter storms.
With every new dawn, there's beauty anew,
Shards of light dancing, forever in view.

Magical Glow in the Winter's Embrace

A tapestry woven with snowflakes and dreams,
Twilight descends with its soft glowing beams.
The air filled with magic, a silent delight,
Wrapped in the warmth of a cozy night.

Trees dressed in white, standing so tall,
Blankets of silence, covering all.
Each breath a vision, each heartbeat a song,
In winter's embrace, we truly belong.

Candles are flickering, casting soft light,
Beneath starlit skies, the world feels just right.
We gather together, hearts open wide,
In this magical glow, we'll forever reside.

As snowflakes keep falling, dreams flutter free,
In the night's gentle hold, just you and me.
Together we wander, enchanted by grace,
In the magical glow, we find our place.

Milton Keynes UK
Ingram Content Group UK Ltd.
UKHW021843151124
451262UK00014B/1287

9 789916 944257